ABOUT THE
LECTIO DIVINA
BIBLE STUDIES

ectio divina, Latin for *divine reading,* is the ancient Christian practice of communicating with God through the reading and study of Scripture. Throughout history, great Christian leaders including John Wesley have used and adapted this ancient method of interpreting Scripture. This Bible study builds on this practice, introducing modern readers of the Bible to the time-honored tradition of "listening for God" through His Word. In this series, the traditional *lectio divina* model has been revised and expanded for use in group Bible study. Each session in this study includes the following elements. (Latin equivalents are noted in italics.)

- Summary   A brief overview of the session.
  Epitome

- Silence   A time of quieting oneself prior to
  Silencio   reading the Word.

- Preparation   Focusing the mind on the central
  Praeparatio   theme of the text.

- Reading   Carefully reading a passage of
  Lectio   Scripture.

- Meditation   Exploring the meaning of the Bible
  Meditatio   passage.

- Contemplation   Yielding oneself to God's will.
  Contemplatio

- Prayer   Expressing praise, thanksgiving,
  Oratio   confession, or agreement to God.

- Incarnation   Resolving to act on the message of
  Incarnatio   Scripture.

The Lectio Divina Bible Studies invite readers to slow down, read Scripture, meditate upon it, and prayerfully respond to God's Word.

LISTENING FOR GOD
THROUGH
REVELATION

Lectio Divina Bible Studies

wph publishing
house

Indianapolis, Indiana

Beacon Hill Press of Kansas City
Kansas City, Missouri

Copyright © 2006 by Wesleyan Publishing House
Published by Wesleyan Publishing House and Beacon Hill Press of Kansas City
Indianapolis, Indiana 46250
Printed in the United States of America

ISBN-13: 978-0-89827-323-6
ISBN-10: 0-89827-323-4

Written by George Lyons.

CONTENTS

INTRODUCTION

I have vivid, youthful memories of traveling evangelists with giant charts of end-times events stretched across the front of the sanctuary. They claimed their predictions were based on the book of "Revelations." If I hadn't been so naïve, I might have reasoned that those who could not even get the title right were probably not as qualified to interpret it as they let on.

These so-called "preachers of good news" played on our contempt for Catholics, our fear of Communism, and our ignorance of Revelation. And, of course, most of their predictions were mistaken. John Kennedy did not turn out to be the Antichrist, after all. Nor did Pope John XXIII or Nikita Khrushchev. The doomsayers had succeeded in turning the imagery of Revelation into the scenery of our nightmares. They turned a book that God intended to encourage first-century believers into a book that scared the devil out of many twentieth-century believers.

But the evangelists were long gone, inflicting their revised theories on some other unsuspecting congregation, before we realized we had been fooled. Eventually, most of us stopped believing self-proclaimed, prophecy experts. Unfortunately, many also stopped reading Revelation.

Today, there is a renewed interest in the book. Popular prophecy books, claiming to have cracked secret codes, fundamentally misunderstand Revelation as the script of history written cryptically in advance. Most believers fail to realize that the most widespread interpretations of Revelation today are relatively young innovations with very little historical support. Despite the claims of contemporary books, the task of readers of Revelation is not to discover the true identity of its characters and events, or to figure out exactly where we are in the countdown to Armageddon.

Rather, the powerful overriding message of Revelation is that since the first coming of Christ, God reigns unchallenged in heaven. And despite appearances to the contrary on earth, God will win in the end. But what are we to do between the times? How should we celebrate God's present reign in heaven as we await His future reign on earth? Revelation challenges us to live holy lives, worship God, sing hymns, and share meals together. In other words, it challenges us to be the Church.

Revelation was not intended to be read alone silently. Don't miss the blessing pronounced on those who read it aloud and on those who hear it read.

ENCOURAGEMENT FOR TOUGH TIMES

Listening for God through Revelation 1:1–20

SUMMARY

These were tough times for the churches of Asia. John was in exile, separated from his churches by forty miles of sea. Both John and his churches were persecuted for preaching the word of God and testifying about Jesus. They were companions in suffering and patient endurance—and in the kingdom of Jesus.

On a Sunday morning, John gazed across the azure Aegean, longing to gather with those he loved. Alone on the Lord's Day, he was in the Spirit.

Read the sidebar on the biblical allusions in Revelation. Does it sound to you as if John's exile deprived him of his Bible?

> In Revelation's 404 verses there are 518 scriptural allusions, but no direct quotations. John is so immersed in Scripture that he does not merely repeat it, it is recreated in him. He does not quote Scripture to prove something; he assimilates it so that he becomes someone.
>
> —Eugene H. Peterson

When John turned to see the voice he had heard behind him, he saw Jesus Christ, the heavenly Son of Man. This revelation changed everything. Jesus really was Lord. He had not lost His voice. And He had good news. His churches were not abandoned. Christ stood among them in resurrection power and glory.

SILENCE ✝ LISTEN FOR GOD

Turn from all that would distract you and hear the voice of the Living One say, "Do not be afraid . . . I hold the keys" (1:17–18).

PREPARATION ✝ FOCUS YOUR THOUGHTS

What present circumstances, or people, challenge your confidence in the lordship of Christ?

Who are you involuntarily separated from? What encouraging messages from Christ do you—and they—need to hear?

Lectio READING ✝ HEAR THE WORD

Many mistakenly have called this the book of Revelation*s*. It is *The Revelation*—singular. It is not a series of predictions about the end of the world. It discloses previously unknown information about Jesus Christ. He is Revelation's central content and primary mediator.

Ancient tradition holds that Revelation was written during a time of intense, state-sanctioned persecution of Christians under the reign of Roman Emperor Domitian (AD 81–96). He promoted emperor worship, requiring even his family to address him as "my lord and my god." But Christ is "the ruler of the kings of the earth" (v. 5). John describes Him as Daniel's heavenly Son of Man (Dan. 7:13–14) and as our High Priest (Zech. 3:1–10). He, not the seven planets of astrology, is Lord of human destiny (v. 16).

Knowing all this, read Revelation 1 aloud.

MEDITATION ✝ ENGAGE THE WORD

Meditate on Revelation 1:1–3

How does John describe himself here? How would you describe yourself in relation to God and other believers?

God revealed Christ to John. Of what use is revelation unless God urges and empowers you to share it (v. 19). How has God revealed Christ to you? How have you shared these insights with others?

What God revealed—"the word of God and the testimony of Jesus Christ"—got John exiled to begin with (see v. 9). Obedience isn't easy. What has God urged you to do that is difficult?

John promises inner happiness to those who read and hear "the words of this prophecy." What does it require not only to "hear," but to "take to heart" the message of this book?

Read the sidebar and the Revelation beatitudes it lists. What blessings do you need from God? What must you do to qualify to receive them?

Revelation 1:3 is the first of seven beatitudes in Revelation. Read the others in 14:13; 16:15; 19:9; 20:6; 22:7, 14.

The Bible seldom uses prophecy for detailed predictions of the distant future. Prophecy is not the script of history written in advance. Prophets offer God's perspective on what He is up to: what He has done in the past, is doing in the present, and is about to do in the near future. What is God doing in your life now to prepare you for the future?

Meditate on Revelation 1:4–8

The risen Christ had a message for *each* of seven Asian churches (2:1–3:22). But John sent the entire script to *all* of them. Read these letters and ask yourself, What is Christ saying to me?

There were other Asian churches. We know of Troas, Colosse, Laodicea, and Hierapolis (2 Cor. 2:12; Col. 1:2; 4:13). The perfect number seven probably symbolized the entire Church, but why might these seven local gatherings of believers have been singled out?

Have you ever read another's mail (with permission, of course)? What are the unique challenges of interpreting a personal letter written to someone else?

Read the Revelation doxologies listed in the next sidebar. What can we learn from Revelation's doxologies?

> The doxology in 1:5 and 6 is the first of seven in Revelation. Read the others in 4:8–11; 5:9–14; 7:10–12; 11:15–18; 15:3–4; 19:1–8.

Note John's special identification of the Triune source of his blessing. How does he describe each person of the Trinity? What does this reveal about God? What does it reveal about us?

The allusions to Daniel and Zechariah (see the sidebars) announce the theme of Revelation: the crucified Christ will return in glory as the exalted Son of Man and triumph over His enemies. Will you mourn or rejoice at His coming?

> And I will pour out on the house of David and the inhabitants of Jerusalem a spirit of grace and supplication. They will look on me, the one they have pierced, and they will mourn for him as one mourns for an only child, and grieve bitterly for him as one grieves for a firstborn son.
>
> —Zechariah 12:10

Meditate on Revelation 1:9–20

What does this portion of Revelation have to say to Christians who have never suffered for their testimony?

The voice who identified Himself as the Almighty Eternal God (1:8; see Isa. 44:6; 48:12) was the crucified, risen, and reigning Christ (1:18; see 19:13). Why did the churches need to recognize that the Sovereign Lord was with them? What difference does it make to you in tough times to know Christ is with you?

> In my vision at night I looked, and there before me was one like a son of man, coming with the clouds of heaven. He approached the Ancient of Days and was led into his presence. He was given authority, glory and sovereign power; all peoples, nations and men of every language worshiped him. His dominion is an everlasting dominion that will not pass away, and his kingdom is one that will never be destroyed.
>
> —Daniel 7:13–14

CONTEMPLATION ✝ REFLECT AND YIELD

To each church Christ said, "He who has an ear, let him hear what the Spirit says to the churches" (2:7, 11, 17; 3:6, 13, 22). If your church is loveless, unrepentant, impoverished, compromising, misguided, lifeless, weak, self-satisfied, and lukewarm; take heart! The heavenly Christ stands among you.

PRAYER ✝ RESPOND TO GOD

Read again Christ's words of reassurance in 1:17–18. What frightens you? Tough times? Separation from loved ones? Suffering? Death? The second coming? Almighty God? Pray that God will help you hear Christ's words of challenge and comfort.

INCARNATION ✝ LIVE THE WORD

Conspire to bless someone by reading them a passage from Revelation this week.

Fulfill your calling as a priest (1:6) by building a bridge connecting the people you care about with God.

WORTHY IS THE LAMB

Listening for God through Revelation 5:1–14

SUMMARY

H ow does God intend to achieve His purposes in our fallen world? How will the forces of rebellion be defeated? How will inadequate churches, like those described in chapters 2 and 3, ever win a beachhead for the rule of God? Revelation's answer to these questions may surprise you: victory is won by the persuasive power of self-sacrificing love. The model for all would-be overcomers is the slain Lamb of God.

"After this I looked" begins the vision in Revelation 4:1 that concludes in 5:14. The setting of the vision is the heavenly throne room (Ezekiel 1–3; Isaiah 6). In chapter 4, God the Father is praised as Creator. In chapter 5, God the Son is praised as Redeemer. The same Greek phrase—translated "Then I saw"

(5:1, 6), "And I saw" (5:2), and "Then I looked" (5:11)—introduces each of the four scenes within chapter five.

SILENCE ✝ LISTEN FOR GOD

Drown the din of earthly noise by joining with the loud song
of heaven. Repeat the phrase, "Worthy is the Lamb, who was
slain," until you hear heaven's amen.

PREPARATION ✝ FOCUS YOUR THOUGHTS

Should we mix religion and politics? How about private faith
with public policy? When (if ever) should pastors preach
about the political implications of the gospel? What are the
dangers of doing so or refraining from doing so?

READING ✝ HEAR THE WORD

John never describes the invisible God in Revelation 4. He
offers only an impression of the splendor (4:3–6) that
surrounds God the Father, who is refered to as "him who sat
on the throne" (5:1). This politically loaded designation insists
that real authority resides in heaven, not in Rome. Consider

how this reminder would have encouraged the first-century readers of this letter.

God's "right hand" (5:1) represents His power to make things happen: creation (Isa. 48:13), exodus (Exod. 15:6, 12), conquest (Ps. 44:3–7), and judgment (Ps. 21:8).

The "twenty-four elders" (5:8) represent glorified believers: Old and New Testament saints, not angels (5:11). All believers are a kingdom of priests (4:4, 10; 5:8–10; 11:16–18; 19:4), in heaven and on earth (1:6; 3:21; 5:10; 20:4, 6).

The "Lion of the tribe of Judah" (5:5; Gen. 49:8–10; Ezekiel 19) and the "Root of David" (5:5; Isa. 11:1–10; Jer. 23:5; Rom. 15:12) are messianic titles. Of course, these figurative images do not describe the Messiah literally; He was a human descendant of Judah, the royal family of David.

Read aloud Revelation 5:1–14.

MEDITATION ✝ ENGAGE THE WORD

Meditate on Revelation 5:1

In chapter 4, heaven's open door gives John a glimpse of the glory and praise of the Creator-God. But, in chapter 5, his attention turns to a sealed scroll in God's right hand. It is filled, but its contents are unknown.

We are never told what the scroll represents. Was it "the book of life" (3:5; 13:8), the Scriptures, or the balance of the message John was to write (1:11)? What do you think?

Does your faith leave room for mystery? Can humans ever fully understand God or the Bible?

When the scroll's seals are removed in 6:1–8:5, its contents are not read; they are enacted. God's twin purposes for the world—redemption and judgment—are accomplished. How do you personally reconcile these two purposes, which seem diametrically opposed to each other?

Meditate on Revelation 5:2–5

Only one person in the entire universe is qualified to execute God's purposes—Jesus Christ. This is true not because of His lineage, but because He triumphed.

Read the sidebar quotation from 2 Corinthians. Do you take seriously the Bible's claim that all of God's purposes and promises are fulfilled in Christ? Should we expect anything more than what God has already given?

> For the Son of God, Jesus Christ, who was preached among you...was not "Yes" and "No," but in him it has always been "Yes." For no matter how many promises God has made, they are "Yes" in Christ.
>
> —2 Corinthians 1:19–20a

Meditate on Revelation 5:6–10

Although John expects to see a Lion (5:5–6), he sees a Lamb. It was slaughtered, but standing and obviously alive. This symbolizes the crucified and risen Christ (Rev. 1:5; 5:9).

How is our appreciation of redemption enhanced by this poetic imagery? Are some things adequately described only as metaphors? If imagery is essential, can prosaic explanations ever replace it? Why do you suppose Revelation uses the images it does to describe Christ?

Read the sidebar on Revelation's Lamb imagery. Do you prefer this imagery or the abstract ideas it represents: the crucified, risen, and reigning Christ as omnipotent, omniscient, and omnipresent? Why?

Christ shares all the prerogatives of God because He is God. How well does the Lion and Lamb image bring a concrete fact to what Paul says in 1 Corinthians 1:23–25—namely that Christ, crucified in weakness, reveals God's strength and realizes His redemptive plan?

> If we take the description of the Lamb literally, the resulting picture of Christ as an animal with ugly scars, seven horns and seven eyes, is a bizarre and repulsive monstrosity. Obviously, we should not see pictures, but look beyond the imagery to its significance. The horns symbolize Christ's power; eyes, His penetrating presence; and the number seven, their fullness.

Read the sidebar about priests. How does the explanation of the imagery in 5:8 help you interpret the roles of other priest-elders? What is your role in this kingdom of priests?

> 1 Chronicles 25 describes the duties of Israel's priests. Like them, the twenty-four elders sing, play musical instruments, and carry censers full of incense.

The bowls of incense are heavenly descriptions of believers' prayers. Do we need a mediator to go before God in prayer, or do we have direct access through Jesus Christ? Explain your answer.

Christ is worthy of universal praise because He is the Redeemer. He set people free at the cost of His life. What does the fourfold description of the reach of His saving work (7:9; 11:9; 13:7; 14:6) suggest about the scope of God's redemptive plan?

If redemption is the costly restoration to the Creator all that is rightfully His, how should the redeemed demonstrate the all-inclusive love of Christ?

Read the sidebar quotation from Revelation 12. If Christ triumphed over evil by self-sacrifice, in what ways are believers to overcome evil and reign with Christ (5:10)? Why should followers of Jesus live as priests now, not just in the future? How do you make room for self-sacrifice in your life?

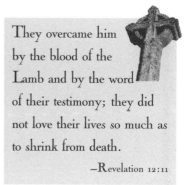

They overcame him by the blood of the Lamb and by the word of their testimony; they did not love their lives so much as to shrink from death.

—Revelation 12:11

Mediate on Revelation 5:11–14

God's people are joined by trillions of angels and all creation in recognizing Christ as fully God and worthy of sevenfold worship. List the seven things described in this passage that are rightly His. How do you respond to the statement that this glimpse of heavenly worship is intended to inspire us to join the song now, not wait until heaven? How can you participate in this worship even now?

CONTEMPLATION ✝ REFLECT AND YIELD

Ask God how you should live as a follower of the worthy Lamb. Have been living the life of a faithful follower of Christ?

Oratio PRAYER ♰ RESPOND TO GOD

Repeat the songs of Revelation 5:9–10, 12, and 13 as prayers of praise to Christ.

Incarnatio INCARNATION ♰ LIVE THE WORD

Strategize how you can become a revolutionary representative of the gospel of self-sacrifice this week. Plan to surrender some of your rights in the interests of redemption. Which will they be?

STANDING IN
TRIBULATION

Listening for God through Revelation 7:1–17

SUMMARY

A s the Lamb opens the first six seals of the scroll (Rev. 5), its
message is enacted (Rev. 6:1–17). Chapter 7 is an interlude
preparing for the opening of the seventh seal (Rev. 8:1–5), which
sets in motion the sounding of seven trumpets (8:6–11:18).

The parallel visions of chapter 7 have nearly identical
introductions, "After this I saw/looked" (7:1, 9). Both assure
God's people of His presence during the plagues of judgment
that are unleashed upon rebellious creation with the opening of
the sealed scroll.

The first vision (7:1–8) narrates the sealing of "the servants of
our God" (7:3). The seal represents divine ownership. The

imagery assures believers that God will protect them *through*, but will *not* spare them *from* tribulation. The second vision (7:9–17) offers a glimpse of the future rewards awaiting the faithful.

SILENCE ✞ LISTEN FOR GOD

Memorize this confession of faith, "Salvation belongs to our God, who sits on the throne, and to the Lamb" (7:10).

PREPARATION ✞ FOCUS YOUR THOUGHTS

How do you respond to the sidebar report by Gailey? Can the deaths of over 150,000 Christians, annually, for their faith so far during the twenty-first century be reconciled with the popular expectation that believers escape great tribulation?

The twentieth century produced more martyrs than the first nineteen centuries of Christian history combined.

—Charles Gailey

Lectio

READING ✝ HEAR THE WORD

The end of Revelation 6 questions who can stand in tribulation (6:17)? Revelation 7 answers: angels and those who worship the Lamb. Despite chaos on earth, heaven's celebration continues undisturbed. Earthbound citizens of heaven are divinely protected—sealed—in the midst of earth's suffering.

Read the sidebar quotation from Peterson. Persecution singles out Christians (6:9–11). But war, catastrophe, scarcity, famine, plague, sickness, and accidents respect no one (6:1–8, 12–17). They impact all indiscriminately, even God's people.

> We are protected from the God-separating effects of evil even as we experience the suffering caused by evil.
>
> —Eugene H. Peterson

The number 12 had special significance for both the old and new covenant communities of God's people—the tribes of Israel and apostles of the church. The identical numbers of each tribe—12,000—and the exclusion of Dan and Ephraim from the list support the conclusion that the 144,000 symbolize spiritual Israel—all God's people. The multitudes in the parallel visions are not different groups, but the same redeemed people. The number was what John heard (7:4); the innumerable multitude, what he saw (7:9).

Read aloud Revelation 7:1–17.

MEDITATION ✝ ENGAGE THE WORD

Meditate on Revelation 7:1–8

How does the explained imagery in Revelation (e.g., 1:20; 5:8; 19:8) give clues as to how the other imagery should be interpreted? Does the symbolic reading of the 144,000 persuade you? What about the figurative explanation of the tribes?

Why should the "seal on the foreheads" (7:3) not be taken literally as a brand or tattoo? How do Romans 4:11 and 1 Corinthians 9:2 help clarify the metaphorical meaning of *seal?*

If the seal refers to the Holy Spirit who guarantees our final salvation (Eph. 1:13–14; 4:30; 2 Cor. 1:21–22), what does He do for suffering Christians? Consult Romans 8 for hints.

How can Christians face tribulation triumphantly? What makes the difference between the overcomers and the overwhelmed?

Meditate on Revelation 7:9–17

How do other passages in Revelation (especially 3:4, 5, 18; 4:4; 5:9; 6:9–11; 7:13–17) help identify the innumerable multitude in 7:9? What do their white robes symbolize? Are these the redeemed of all ages or the martyrs of the final age? Is this a vision of the future, or the present seen from heaven's perspective? How do you support your answers?

Read the apocryphal quotation about Israel's celebration of the defeat of their second-century BC persecutors. How does this help explain the symbolism of palms here?

> [They] entered [Jerusalem] with praise and palm branches, and with harps and cymbals and stringed instruments, and with hymns and songs, because a great enemy had been crushed and removed from Israel.
>
> —1 Maccabees 13:51 (New Revised Standard Version Apocrypha)

According to 7:10, the redeemed continually praise the Source of their salvation. What does their joint worship of the Father and the Son here (and in 12:10 and 19:1) imply?

Consider 7:12 and 5:12 in light of the sidebar about doxology. Do we glorify God to prop up His fragile ego or to remind ourselves of who He really is? Explain your answer.

The English word doxology comes from the Greek word, doxa, meaning glory. One who possesses glory has an impressive reputation. He must be reckoned with. He has an aura of majesty—a certain radiance—about Him. Glory is not something creatures give God that He does not already possess; it is something they recognize about Him.

Christ's death qualifies the redeemed to serve God day and night in His temple. But if there is no temple and no night in the eternal city (21:22–27), where and when do the redeemed serve? How do the redeemed fulfill their priestly role? Explain your answer.

The present tense suggests that believers serve God now. The future tense describes what God *will do* to reward the faithful in the future. The present tense in 7:14 and 15:2 suggests that great tribulation and conquering the beast are ongoing and repeated experiences of the church. Would John's original readers have ever imagined only nonbelievers of some distant future era suffering tribulation? Given their experience, would they have expected the redeemed to escape great tribulation? How do your answers support or challenge popular Christian expectations of the end times?

Does our comfort suggest that we are especially favored by God or that our faith is deficient? Is undeserved suffering from natural catastrophes, cancer, etc. an aspect of great tribulation? How do you defend your views?

From what will the future deliverance of the redeemed bring relief? (Read 7:15b–17 for hints.)

God is already on the throne. God—not Rome—is the center of authority in the world, despite appearances to the contrary. This imagery of the tent alludes to the tabernacle where God made His presence known to Israel in the wilderness. What comfort is there in the promise that God "will spread his tent over" the suffering redeemed, but not exempt them from suffering?

CONTEMPLATION ✝ REFLECT AND YIELD

How does reading Revelation 7 as heaven's perspective on the life and ministry of redeemed people change your outlook on the Christian life?

Is God calling you to take a daunting step of faith, to do something at which you will fail unless He assists you?

Prayer ✝ Respond to God

For what tribulations—great or small—do you need God's seal now? Seek God's guidance as to how you can best serve the persecuted church.

Incarnation ✝ Live the Word

Visit the Web sites http://www.persecution.org and http://www.persecution.com to learn about persecuted Christians and what you can do about it.

Volunteer to serve in a Christian relief agency in your community.

JUDGMENT AND REDEMPTION

Listening for God through Revelation 11:15–12:12

SUMMARY

Judgment is the essential counterpart of redemption. For example, God's deliverance of Israel from slavery meant judgment for their Egyptian oppressors. Biblical justice demands that those who live by the sword will die by the sword (Matt. 26:52; Rev. 13:10). Punishment is in kind (2 Thess. 1:6). Judgment destroys those who destroy (11:18).

Biblical judgment also discloses God's holy revulsion against evil. His wrath is motivated not by vengeance but by His desire that sinners repent (Rom. 2:1–11). Sadly, most refuse (Rev. 9:20–21; 16:9–11), and thus are subject to an eternal doom that is as horrendous as it is final.

SILENCE ✝ LISTEN FOR GOD

Recall the inspiring music of Handel's "Hallelujah Chorus." Stand for a few moments in silent awe of the King of kings and Lord of lords.

PREPARATION ✝ FOCUS YOUR THOUGHTS

Could heaven exist without hell? What would become of heaven if evil were allowed there? How can God deal with unrepentant humans without violating their freedom?

READING ✝ HEAR THE WORD

When the seventh seal (6:1–8:5) was opened "there was silence in heaven" (8:1). But when the seventh trumpet (8:6–11:18) sounded "there were loud voices in heaven" (11:15). The voices announced, "The kingdom of the world has become the kingdom of our Lord and of his Christ, and he will reign for ever and ever" (11:15).

Revelation 11–15 employs lavish imagery to explain repeatedly how God asserted His right to rule and how the consequences of His rule unfold. Its dramatic impact is best experienced by reading it aloud.

Like the seals, the seven trumpets trigger earthly events. The first six bring plagues resembling those of Egypt. But this time God achieves victory not by the death of the oppressors' first-born but by the death of His firstborn. When God becomes accessible to all, the cosmos reels, and the new age dawns.

Revelation 12 parodies Roman mythology to tell how God's reign became reality. A heavenly woman gives birth. The newborn Messiah is rescued as the dragon prepares to devour Him (12:1–6). The dragon redirects his fury against the woman and her children.

Read aloud Revelation 11:15–12:12. If time permits, continue through 15:4.

MEDITATION ✝ ENGAGE THE WORD

Meditate on Revelation 11:15–19

God rules now. While this is good news for Christians, it spells disaster for evil and the Devil (11:14, 18). Cite some examples of times when the same news could be interpreted as good or bad, depending on the audience.

Most Jews believed the present age was under Satan's control. God's rule awaited the distant future. Revelation insists that the new age has dawned already, although the darkness of the old age lingers.

What is implied by the transposition of the description of God first as the One "who was, and is, and is to come" (1:4, 8; 4:8), and now in Revelation 11:6–7 as "the One who is, and who was, and who is to come"?

With Christ's coming, God has exercised His sovereignty (11:17–18). The future is now. What evidence can you cite to suggest that this passage refers to the first rather than the second coming of Christ, that God reigns now, and that God is now accessible to all?

Read the sidebar quotation from John. In what sense are the living already saved or judged? Are deceased believers already receiving their eternal reward? Are the unrepentant dead already being punished?

> For God did not send the Son into the world to judge the world, but that the world might be saved through Him. He who believes in Him is not judged; he who does not believe has been judged already, because he has not believed in the name of the only begotten Son of God.
>
> —John 3:17–18, NASB

Why are some Christians ambivalent about the doctrine of hell? What dangers result from overemphasizing divine judgment? What dangers result from neglecting it? What is the proper balance?

Meditate on Revelation 12:1–12

Read the sidebar about ancient combat myths. What other Christian adaptations of cultural stories have served as media of the gospel? (Consider Lewis's *Chronicles of Narnia* as one example.)

The Messiah is only apparently uninvolved in the heavenly combat because this combat actually symbolizes the earthly battle waged at the Cross (12:7, 10; 13:8). The archangel Michael (Dan. 10:13) leads the forces of God against the dragon. Like this great spiritual and physical war, do our current battles have heavenly counterparts? Read Ephesians 6:10–20 and then revisit your answer.

Roman emperors sometimes exploited ancient myths of divine combat to claim they were savior-gods, sons of the goddess Roma, pursued by sinister dragons that complicated their efforts to usher in an era of peace. Revelation 12 parodies such myths to lampoon Rome. Christ, not the emperor, launched the golden age. Rome was a doomed prostitute (16–17), not queen of heaven. The emperor, far from a savior, was a beastly agent of Satan (13).

Read the sidebar on Satan's role in the Old Testament era as accuser of God's people. How does it make you feel to know that God wins! Satan and his minions are defeated and expelled from heaven (12:8–10; Luke 10:18; John 12:31). God rules unchallenged in heaven. Now!

In the Old Testament, Satan's appearance in the heavenly council alongside other angelic beings was taken for granted (Job 1:6–11; 2:4–5; Zech. 3:1). His divinely authorized function, like that of an investigative detective and a prosecuting attorney, was to test the faithfulness of God's people. We can only guess how the accuser became a sinister rebel against God, intent on destroying the relationship between God and His people.

Likewise, the suffering victims of Satan's accusations and the heavenly martyrs (6:6–9) also win. They overcame Satan (12:11). But since rebellion continues and suffering only intensifies (12:12, 17), how can John claim that God and persecuted saints triumph?

The victory of God's people looks like defeat to the world, because their victory, like their Lord's, comes by self-sacrifice (7:14). Read the sidebar on martyrs. What is required of faithful witnesses today? How are you an overcomer?

The Greek word martys means "witness," one who speaks the truth based on personal experience. But speaking the truth about God in an evil world can be difficult and dangerous. Faithful witnesses are sometimes killed for telling the truth. They do not seek death; but they do not shrink from it either. Thus, martys has come into English as martyr, one who dies for the faith.

Charged by Rome and convicted of the crime of being Christians, Asian believers were ultimately and eternally acquitted in heaven. Their testimony consisted not only of bold words, but also of innocent suffering (14:13). How do you respond to the sidebar quotation by Bill Draper?

If you were charged with being a Christian, would there be enough evidence to convict you?

–Bill Draper

Remember heaven's song is both good news and bad news. Christ's enthronement as king brings both salvation and disaster (12:12). Heaven's victory is not yet an earthly reality. For now, Satan's defeat only makes matters worse on earth. But his days are numbered.

CONTEMPLATION ✝ REFLECT AND YIELD

How is the paradox of victory and self-sacrifice expressed in your life?

How does the extravagant imagery of Revelation provide a new handle for thinking about the "already, but not yet" paradox?

PRAYER ✝ RESPOND TO GOD

Paul and John agree. "The God of peace will soon crush Satan under your feet" (Rom. 16:20). "He gives us the victory through our Lord Jesus Christ" (1 Cor. 15:57). Thank God for the victory that is yours *now* as you serve Christ.

INCARNATION ✝ LIVE THE WORD

Put the last volume of C. S. Lewis's *Chronicles of Narnia—The Final Battle*—on your must-read list for this year.

Find an opportunity to tell the truth about God this week to someone deceived by the father of lies (John 8:44).

A Tale of
Two Feasts

Listening for God through Revelation 19:1–21

Summary

How should we celebrate God's present reign in heaven and future reign on earth? How about with victory songs and a banquet?

Revelation 19 is intelligible only within its larger context, 17:1–19:21. Here Rome, alias Babylon, is pictured as a great prostitute, condemned for seducing people to worship the beast Emperor.

Babylon's impending doom sets the stage for God's universal sovereignty (11:15–19). The prospect of judgment assured John's readers that God would destroy the destroyers of the earth (11:18) and make it a fit place for His reign.

The hymns of the twenty-four elders in Revelation 11 proclaim that it is the time to reward the faithful and punish the wicked. In Revelation 19 the reward of the faithful consists in an invitation to attend the wedding supper of the Lamb as both bride and guest. The punishment of the wicked, too, is a feast. But it is a grisly feast in which *they* are the menu and the guests.

SILENCE ✝ LISTEN FOR GOD

Flee the noise of "Babble-on" (18:4) and find a place where you can hear "the true words of God" (19:9).

PREPARATION ✝ FOCUS YOUR THOUGHTS

What's your favorite meal? If you could share this meal with several other believers of any time in history, who would you choose? What would you talk about over dinner?

READING ✝ HEAR THE WORD

John heard the innumerable throng of the redeemed singing victory songs (chapters 7 and 14), celebrating Babylon's doom (chapter 18). They represent all God's servants, small and great (19:5).

Their song begins with the Hebrew call to worship, "Hallelujah!" Frequent in Psalms, the word appears in the New Testament only in Revelation 19. They praise the Lord God Almighty because He reigns (19:6).

Revelation 19 celebrates salvation as a communal meal. Judgment takes the form of "the great supper of God," a banquet of consequences for rebellion against God, in which evil self-destructs.

Christ's victory over evil also involves the capture and destruction of the beast and the false prophet (19:20; and chapters 13, 14, 16, and 17).

Read aloud Revelation 19:1–21.

MEDITATION ✝ ENGAGE THE WORD

Meditate on Revelation 19:1–5

Because Rome reprised the role of Babylon (the evil empire bent on destroying God's people), its destruction was inevitable. What later nations made themselves enemies of God's true servants? How did they come to ruin? What nations today face judgment unless they repent?

The destruction of Babylon is evidence of God's impressive ability to save His beleaguered servants and that His judgment of evil is truly just and worthy of praise (19:1). Are you confident of God's commitment to justice and competence to judge? How can God's love be reconciled with His contempt for injustice? How can you appropriately fear God today?

Meditate on Revelation 19:6–10

The tumultuous song of the redeemed overpowers all other sounds (19:6–7). Why are some Christians quiet about their praise? What are some ways you can put more joy into your praise?

The multitude praised God because the wedding supper of the Lamb and the bride were ready (19:7–9). Read the sidebar on wedding imagery. How suitable is marriage today as an image for the relationship between Christ and the church?

The wedding as a symbol of God's earthly reign is developed in Revelation 21:1–22:5. The imagery of the Church as the "bride of Christ" also appears in Matt. 22:1–14; Mark 2:19–20; 2 Cor. 11:2; and Eph. 5:22–32. Old Testament prophets used marriage to describe the covenant relationship between God and His people. (See Hos. 2:16–22; Isa. 54:5–6; 62:5; Jer. 2:2; Eze. 16:6–14.)

The bride's readiness was symbolized by her gown (19:8). Read the sidebar about holiness and clean garments. How do you respond to the symbolism of Christian holiness as donning clothing? How apt is this example in today's world?

> Clean garments often symbolize holiness in the Bible. For examples, read Genesis 35:2; Isaiah 52:1; Matthew 22:1–14; Ephesians 4:22–5:2; and Revelation 3:4–5.

How do you respond to the Eugene Peterson's definition of holiness in the sidebar? How can we avoid thinking about holiness as either divine magic or the result of human effort?

John mixes his metaphors. The wedding gown represents both Christ's gift of holiness and the righteous deeds His people do (Eph. 2:8–10; Phil. 2:12–13). The Church is both the bride and the invited guest (19:9).

> Holy living is the action by which we express in our behavior and speech the love and presence of our Christ.
> —Eugene H. Peterson

Discuss why no image can adequately explain spiritual realities. Why can we never understand spiritual realities without some kind of imagery?

The wedding supper celebrates the union of Christ and His Church. Read the sidebar cross references. How may we anticipate this communion meal when we observe the Lord's Supper? (See also Matt. 26:29 and Rev. 3:20.)

> In biblical imagery a wedding banquet frequently symbolizes the Kingdom of God. Look up Isaiah 25:6; Matthew 22:1–14; Mark 14:25; and Luke 14:15–24.

Meditate on Revelation 19:11–21

Scan or read Ezekiel 38–39. How did this prophecy influence John's description of the second coming and the fate of the unrepentant?

Revelation reports no battle, despite the combat imagery. What evidence suggests that the second coming only seals the victory already won at the cross?

Christ's robe is covered with His blood before the battle begins (19:13). He overpowers evil with His self-sacrificing love. What evidence suggests that persuasive preaching is His only weapon (19:21; 2 Cor. 10:1–6; Eph. 6:10–20)? What modern examples of non-violent resistance illustrate how the message and incarnation of self-sacrificing love can still defeat evil?

Revelation 19:17–18 uses the crass imagery of the grisly feast of Ezekiel 39 to visualize judgment as the self-destructiveness of evil. This would seem to indicate that evil is like a cancer that destroys itself. What do you think of this analogy?

The beast embodies the political powers that try to usurp God's sovereignty. The false prophet represents civil religion and its perverse value systems and social structures that turn people away from worshiping the true God. John's first readers would have identified these symbols with the Roman Emperor and the Asian imperial priesthood. Have later generations of readers correctly identified the beast with similar anti-God pretenders? Cite historical or contemporary examples of this kind of beast. What value systems and social structures are false prophets that turn people away from God today?

CONTEMPLATION ✝ REFLECT AND YIELD

Have you offered yourself as a living sacrifice to God (Rom. 12:1–2)? Have you invited Him to sanctify you so that you may serve as a weapon of righteousness (Romans 6) in His battle to bring the rebellious world to its knees before it destroys itself?

PRAYER ✝ RESPOND TO GOD

Ask God to enable you to live a life of holiness marked by self-sacrificing love. Trust the promise of 1 Thessalonians 5:23–24: "He will do it."

INCARNATION ✝ LIVE THE WORD

Look forward to the next observance of the sacrament of Holy Communion in your church as a foretaste of the heavenly banquet prepared for God's holy people.

Find an opportunity to share the illustration of sin as a self-destructive cancer with a friend who struggles comprehending how a loving God can allow judgment.

HERE COMES THE BRIDE!

Listening for God through Revelation 21:1–21

SUMMARY

John's vision of the Christian's hope challenges popular imaginations about heaven. People don't go up there; heaven comes down here. Not everyone will enter there, only God's holy people—the redeemed from every race and social class.

John's vision intends to strengthen our resolve to reject the values of the world order dominated by Babylon. His language cannot be taken literally. But if this is only imagery, what must the reality be like?

Heaven is not a glorified projection of a consumer paradise where every human craving is gratified. The perverse values of Babylon have no place in God's new order, where gold is so insignificant they pave streets with it (Rev. 21:21).

Encouraging to marginalized first-century Christians, John's vision of heaven may trouble those who want conspicuous consumption and heaven too. God's presence, not abundant riches, makes everything new in the Holy City.

SILENCE ✝ LISTEN FOR GOD

Recall the strains of the traditional wedding march. Allow memories of beautiful weddings to prepare you to contemplate the marriage of the Lamb and His Bride, the Church.

PREPARATION ✝ FOCUS YOUR THOUGHTS

Why do most of us still have sentimental feelings about weddings, despite our awareness that about half of them today end tragically in divorce?

READING ✝ HEAR THE WORD

John's description of the bride-city cannot be taken literally. What a bride! What a city! Fifteen-hundred miles on each side, this cube could never fit in the land of Israel, which is only 70 by 150 miles.

The realization of Isaiah's vision of a new heaven and a new earth (Isa. 65:17–25; 66:22; Rom. 8:19–21) means not the end of the created order, but its recreation. Absent in the new order will be rebellion, unrest, turmoil, chaos, separation, death, mourning, crying, pain, evil, and night (Rev. 21:1, 4; 22:3, 5). God's new order will be "the home of righteousness" (2 Pet. 3:13)—a fit place for a holy God and His holy people to live together in intimate fellowship.

Picturesque language should lead us not to check our calculators but to contemplate the magnitude and attractiveness of the church God intends to unite out of all nations. The cube symbolizes the Holy City's perfection (1 Kings 6:19– 20).

John's dimensions are all multiples of twelve—the symbolic number of Israel's tribes and of the apostles of Christ. No community more is more complete than heaven—nothing is excluded except what is not holy.

Read aloud Revelation 21:1–21.

MEDITATION ✝ ENGAGE THE WORD

Meditate on Revelation 21:1–4 and 9–21

The beautiful Aegean Sea separated John from his churches. The sea was the home of the dragon and the beast (chapter 13). Read the sidebar on sea symbolism. In what other biblical passages does the sea function negatively? John envisioned this sea disappearing in the new order. But John also saw a life-giving sea flowing from the throne of God (4:6; 22:1).

Wherever the images of chaos (confusion, disorder, meaninglessness and formlessness) are present in Scripture, they are uniformly understood as standing in opposition to God and His creation purposes. Thus even an archetypal image like the sea, which represents chaos in ancient Near Eastern mythology and world literature in general, takes on an added significance in the Bible precisely because of its tie to creation.

–Leland Ryken, James C. Wilhoit, Tremper Longman III

What does *sea* represent to you? How do you feel when you recall waves on a beach? How about when you think of a tsunami? Water can both refresh and drown. How do your experiences affect the way you think about this natural order?

Explain what emotions you associate with the following terms: *city, urban sprawl, rush hour, ghetto, suburb, shopping mall, nature preserve, national park, amusement park, desert,* and *forest.* How do your life experiences affect the way you think about such things?

Read the sidebar on city imagery. John's description of the Holy City borrows its imagery from Ezekiel 40–48. This urban vision of God's new order differs markedly from Isaiah 11's vision of paradise as nature rid of the violent struggle for survival. How is the Holy City an apt image of God's pres-

In biblical imagery the city can represent community, safety, and civilization (as in Psa. 107:4–9). But cities can also represent human arrogance, rebellion, perversion, and violence (as in Sodom and Gomorrah, Nineveh, Babylon, and even Jerusalem).

ence with His people? Why might some prefer Isaiah's imagery?

The angel who showed John Babylon's destruction (17:1) invited him to see the unveiling of its replacement, the Holy City. What do you think of the view that the names on the City's twelve gates and twelve foundations mean the church includes all God's people of all time?

What is the symbolic significance of the detailed description of the Holy City? Of what use could a 200-foot-tall wall with open gates (21:17, 25) have for a 1,500-mile-high city? In Revelation 11:1–3, measuring symbolizes God's protection. Could this help explain the measuring of the Holy City?

How can God's eternal dwelling place be like both a city and a beautiful bride? How should we connect the bride imagery here with that in Revelation 19:7–9? How will God live with His people in the new order differently than He is already living with them now? In what sense can the church come down out of heaven from God?

React to the statement in the sidebar about considering heaven as a community of eternal love. Do you agree or disagree with this statement? Why do you suppose some Christians struggle with the

> The imagery of Revelation suggests that heaven should not be thought of primarily as a place, but as a community of eternal love.

thought of heaven as sorrow-free and the awareness that some of their loved ones will be eternally separated from God's love?

Meditate on Revelation 21:5-8

God's assurance "I am making everything new!" alludes to Isaiah 43:19. Does the present tense suggest that the new creation has already begun? Read Romans 8:18-25. What trials of the old order might actually be birth pangs announcing the coming of the new?

Read the Caird quote. It would indicate that God is the source and destination of all that exists, the hidden object and real satisfaction of all human striving. Put this in your own words, and explain why you agree or disagree.

> G. B. Caird explained God's self-description in Revelation 21:6 with the comment: "The end is not an event but a person." The Apostle Paul made a similar claim, "From him and through him and to him are all things" (Rom. 11:36). In the end, God will be "all in all" (1 Cor. 15:28).

Done! The fulfillment of God's promise brings history to its consummation. The church triumphant consists of those who overcome (21:7; 2:7, 17, 26; 3:5, 21). How satisfied would you be if your heavenly inheritance were not material wealth but God Himself?

Heaven is not for everyone. Why will only the holy be there? Why are sin and sinners unwelcome in heaven? How could 21:8 serve as a warning to Christians tempted to deny Christ in times of trial?

CONTEMPLATION ✝ REFLECT AND YIELD

Are you committed to the values and priorities of God's new order?

Take a personal inventory based on how you spend your time and money. Are you ready for the wedding?

PRAYER ✝ RESPOND TO GOD

What is Christ doing in your church to prepare you to be His radiant-bride community? What new thing is God doing in your life? Pray that God will help you make Him the true object of all your strivings.

Incarnation ☩ Live the Word

Are you open to God doing something new in your life? Make yourself accountable to trusted Christian friends who will agree to help you remain faithful to heaven's values and priorities.

No More Night

Listening for God through Revelation 21:22–22:5

Summary

As John continues his description of the bride city, keep in mind that this is not a real estate sales pitch for a fanciful place like Utopia. These are metaphorical images of the church as God intends it to be for eternity.

Twice, John tells us there will be no more night (21:25; 22:5); God will illuminate everything. There is nothing to fear, nothing impure, nothing shameful in the homes of the holy. God alone will be the source of eternal life, perfect health, and unending blessing.

The entire Holy City is a sanctuary. Its citizens— all priests (1:6)—are wholly committed to the worship and service of God. God's immediate presence permeates the bride city.

Silence ✝ Listen for God

Repeat the opening line of Psalm 27: "The Lord is my light and my salvation—whom shall I fear?"

Preparation ✝ Focus Your Thoughts

Share an experience—whether yours or another's—of being afraid of the dark. Why does this seem to be a universal human fear?

Reading ✝ Hear the Word

That there is not a temple in the Holy City does not contradict earlier passages that refer to God's dwelling as a heavenly temple. The entire Holy City *is* the heavenly temple.

John does not say there is no sun, moon, or lamp in God's new order, only that they are superfluous. In biblical imagery light symbolizes the saving revelation of God. How does

Now we see but a poor reflection as in a mirror; then we shall see face to face. Now I know in part; then I shall know fully, even as I am fully known.

—1 Corinthians 13:12

the sidebar quotation from 1 Corinthians illuminate this?

The destruction of the nations (11:18; 19:15) and their kings (19:17–21) would make Revelation 21:24 and 26 impossible, were this not figurative language. The church will teach the nations how to live (21:26; 5:9; 7:10; 15:4). God will not destroy the old order, but transform it. Nothing is excluded from the city except what is not holy (21:27).

God will restore human life to His creation intentions, revoking the ancient curse (22:3). In the imagery of the tree and river of life, God is the source and sustainer of eternal life.

The impossibility of seeing God in the old order will surrender in the new to the full awareness of His presence and power. God's people will be secure and share in His eternal rule.

Read aloud Revelation 21:22–22:5.

MEDITATION ✝ ENGAGE THE WORD

Meditate on Revelation 21:22–27

As you consider this passage of Revelation, read Isaiah 60. How did it shape John's description? How may we fill our minds with the Scriptures so that they may similarly influence our speech?

Read the quote from David Aune. His three-volume commentary on Revelation never answers his question. What is your answer?

Tony Campolo claims many Christians suffer from an "edifice complex"—they associate the church too closely with buildings and institutional structures. Explain your agreement or disagreement after reading the sidebar excerpt from John 4.

> While the notion of a heavenly…Jerusalem was widespread in early Judaism…, John is unique in claiming that there will be no temple within it. It is important to ask why he emphasizes this fact when he…connect[s] the temple of God with the New Jerusalem (3:12; see 7:15), refers often to the temple in heaven (11:19; 14:15, 17; 15:5, 6, 8; 16:1, 17), and uses temple imagery…in descriptions of the heavenly throne room."
>
> —David E. Aune

What does true worship involve, if it is less about a place than about a person? Why are temples necessary in this present age?

Has the remoteness or distance of God affected you? Have you known Christians who have experienced a dark night of the soul? How did they survive until God's presence became real again?

Why do you suppose John repeated the theme that the Holy City needs no "light of the sun" or lamps (21:23 and 22:5), God will illuminate the city (21:23 and 22:5), and there will be no more night (21:25 and 22:5)?

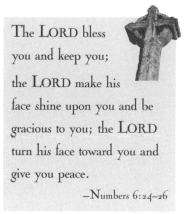

A time is coming when you will worship the Father neither on this mountain nor in Jerusalem…a time is coming and has now come when the true worshipers will worship the Father in spirit and truth, for they are the kind of worshipers the Father seeks. God is spirit, and his worshipers must worship in spirit and in truth."

—John 4:21–24

How does the Aaronic blessing in the sidebar from the book of Numbers affect your answer to the previous question? What do God's presence and blessing reveal about Him?

The LORD bless you and keep you; the LORD make his face shine upon you and be gracious to you; the LORD turn his face toward you and give you peace.

—Numbers 6:24–26

Read the sidebar on Isaiah 60:3. John associates the passage with the eternal city. List examples of the splendor, glory, and honor of the nations (such as certain timeless musical creations) you expect God to preserve in the new order.

According to 21:8, 27 and 22:15, what practices exclude the unrepentant from heaven? What other biblical vice-lists (like Gal. 5:19–21) do you recall? What would heaven be like if vices such as these were allowed?

Some early Christians saw the gifts of the magi to the Christ child in Matthew 2 as fulfilling the prophecy of Isaiah 60:3 and following. This shaped the tradition of the "three kings." Others saw Isaiah's expectations fulfilled in the conversion of Gentiles. Still others associated it with a typological understanding of "the plundering of Egypt" at the Exodus. Convinced that all truth was God's truth, they mined the wisdom of pagan philosophers for insights that advanced the gospel.

Read Revelation's references to the Book of Life—3:5; 13:8; 17:8; 20:12, 15; 21:27. Explain why a heavenly list of the saved (Exod. 32:32) supports either predestination or the necessity of continuing fidelity to God for final salvation.

Meditate on Revelation 22:1–5

Read Ezekiel 47:1–12, and comment on how this passage may have influenced John's description?

Respond to each of the following observations: Eastern Christianity emphasizes growth in holiness throughout eternity. Revelation promises that God will perfectly nourish our progress. True holiness is not stifling or static, but stimulating and dynamic. What Scripture passages would support your position on these observations?

Consider where you turn when you are spiritually dehydrated and malnourished. Then read Revelation's references to the tree of life: 2:7; 22:2, 14, 19. List twelve fruits that nourish your spiritual formation. Why is there no fast food in heaven?

Besides the physical, what other human ills will God heal only in eternity?

Heaven cannot be an eternal vacation, for its residents are servants who share in God's reign. How does this statement challenge popular thinking? How does it cause you to change your own thoughts and anticipation about living there for eternity?

Read Revelation 1:6; 5:10; 20:6; and 22:5. Would you prefer fulfilling work or endless leisure in the new order? Why?

If we will see God in heaven, will He be no longer invisible or will we acquire new eyes? How are we blinded to spiritual realities by the night we mistake for light?

CONTEMPLATION ✝ REFLECT AND YIELD

Does anything of the night still cling to you? Are there any impure, shameful, or deceitful thoughts or actions you need to let God illuminate and eliminate from your life?

PRAYER ✝ RESPOND TO GOD

Pray that God will enable you to see Him, despite the night that sometimes blinds us to what He is already doing to make everything new.

Incarnation ✝ Live the Word

Ephesians 5:11 exhorts, "Have nothing to do with the fruitless deeds of darkness, but rather expose them." How long has it been since you expressed moral outrage about the darkness of this age? Do so in a tangible way this week.

Come, Lord Jesus

Listening for God through Revelation 22:6–21

Summary

Three times the epilogue of Revelation reports the words of Jesus, "I am coming soon!" (22:7, 12, 20). This "must soon take place" (22:6), "because the time is near" (22:10). Two millennia later it seems impossible to understand this as literally referring to the end of the world. If this is what John intended, he was mistaken.

So is Revelation irrelevant? Or does the church still risk its right to the tree of life by compromising with fallen Babylon?

Have we lost the vision of Father Abraham, who "was looking forward to the city with foundations, whose architect and builder is God" (Heb. 11:10)? Were those who died looking

forward to the coming of Christ misguided fools who stead-
fastly refused to trade the next world for a larger stake in this
present world? Revelation answers with a resounding, "No."

SILENCE ✝ LISTEN FOR GOD

Silently prepare yourself to receive the blessing promised
those who read aloud, hear, and heed the message of
Revelation.

PREPARATION ✝ FOCUS YOUR THOUGHTS

Recall a time when you were really thirsty. How was your
thirst eventually quenched? Is your craving for God anything
like such a thirst?

READING ✝ HEAR THE WORD

Christ pronounces the blessing of a happy future on those who
prepare for His coming by heeding Revelation's warnings:
repent of known sin, live a holy life, don't compromise with
the world, and worship God alone.

In Revelation's seventh beatitude, Christ blesses the redeemed who keep their robes clean. The present tense emphasizes that conversion alone is insufficient. The present crisis calls for ongoing faithfulness to the slain Lamb if we are to have eternal life.

These blessings stand in stark contrast to the somber warning of Revelation 22:11. Prophets normally urge people to repent. This verse seems to urge them to remain unchanged. In fact, it warns those who delay repenting that, over time, behaviors become habitual and change becomes impossible. But as long as the door of opportunity remains ajar, there is time to repent.

Read aloud Revelation 22:6–21.

MEDITATION ✝ ENGAGE THE WORD

Meditate on Revelation 22:6–11

How are the words of Revelation "trustworthy and true" (22:6)? How do you reconcile a high view of Scripture with Revelation's apparently failed prediction of Christ's *soon* return? Explain whether you consider this a real issue or only a red herring.

Define the word *soon* in 22:6, 7, 12, 20. How might translating *soon* as *quickly, suddenly,* or *unexpectedly* solve the problem?

How does the sidebar on Domitian's death help solve the problem of apparently failed prophecy? Read 2 Peter 3. How does it help you make sense of this apparent dichotomy?

Within a year of the Revelation's appearance, the Roman Emperor Domitian died and the persecution of Asian Christians ended. Revelation offered them meaningful and timely good news that they would soon be delivered from their troubles. Its first intention was to strengthen and encourage them (13:10; 14:12), not to predict the end of the world. And its prophecy was partially fulfilled in their days.

All who prepared for the second coming and died without experiencing it came to the end of their personal worlds. Unless Jesus comes first, we too will die. How does this insight help?

Consult other translations for help with the meaning of *keeping* the words of Revelation (22:7). What behaviors demonstrate that we are following the prophecy's instructions?

Worship is the central emphasis of Revelation. To worship God is already to participate in the life of heaven. Every glimpse of heaven in Revelation is a scene of worship. Summarize your reading of 4:10; 5:14; 7:11; 11:1, 16; 14:7; 15:4; and 19:4. Why do all Christians need the reminder to worship God?

Read the sidebars on Daniel and the relevance of Revelation. Was John mistaken about the relevance of Revelation for his first readers? Did he misunderstand, or have recent interpreters misunderstood Revelation? Defend your answer.

Daniel was told "seal up the vision, for it concerns the distant future" (Dan. 8:26; see 10:14), "the time of the end" (Dan. 12:4, 9). But John was told, "Do not seal up the words of the prophecy of this book, because the time is near" (Rev. 22:10).

Evaluate this paraphrase of Revelation 22:11, "The older people get, the more like themselves they become." Cynical young men become grouchy old men. If we don't change now, we will become a caricature of our worst-self. Cite examples illustrating this. Which of the options listed in verse 11 would you like to pursue from now until the end of your life? How do you intend to work toward that eventuality?

To insist that Revelation was meaningful to its first readers is not to suggest that it has nothing to say to modern readers. Paul's letters were similarly addressed to real churches and are still relevant to us. Christians today can take heart that now, as then, God triumphs over evil.

Meditate on Revelation 22:12–15

How do you reconcile salvation by faith (e.g., Eph. 2:8) with judgment based on works (Rev. 22:12; 20:13; Matt. 7:21; Rom. 2:6–13; Jas. 2:14–17)?

White robes are the uniform of the redeemed in Revelation 3:4–5, 18; 4:4; 6:11; 7:9, 13, 14; 19:7–8; and 22:14. Read these passages and the sidebar quotations from 1 John and Hebrews. Offer reasons for believing that washing our robes means letting God continue His moral cleansing in our lives.

> But if we walk in the light, as he is in the light, we have fellowship with one another, and the blood of Jesus, his Son, purifies us from all sin.
> —1 John 1:7

> And so Jesus also suffered outside the city gate to make the people holy through his own blood.
> —Hebrews 13:12

Was the list of seven vices excluding people from the Holy City in 22:15 likely posted in the public squares of Asia? What does it imply if this warning is for the churches?

Do we really believe people are either inside or outside the saved community? How should this affect the way we relate to outsiders?

Meditate on Revelation 22:16–21

"Come!" in 22:17 is not a prayer for Christ's return (as in 22:20), but an invitation for all to accept His gracious offer of salvation. Salvation is free, but its price was not cheap. You've heard the invitation and responded for yourself; but now, to whom must you say, "Come!"?

The warning in 22:18–19 led John Calvin to not include a volume on Revelation in his Bible commentary. Surely this was not intended to discourage people from trying to understand the book or from assisting others' efforts. What do you think the Revelator really meant?

Revelation's closing prayer, "Come, Lord Jesus," translates an Aramaic formula from the earliest church: *Maranatha* (also seen in 1 Cor. 16:22). Why did early Christians repeat this prayer whenever they celebrated communion? What would it mean to us today to add this phrase to our communion remembrances?

CONTEMPLATION ✦ REFLECT AND YIELD

How will you heed the words of this prophecy? Are there things about your life you need to ask God to help you change before it is too late? Will you covenant with Him to make changes in your life as a result of what you now know?

PRAYER ✦ RESPOND TO GOD

Join with the saints across twenty centuries in the prayer, "Amen. Come, Lord Jesus." Let God whisper to you the name of one who needs to hear the invitation to come to the table of salvation.

INCARNATION ✦ LIVE THE WORD

Now that you have studied selections of Revelation, set aside a time to read the entire book in one sitting. Don't try to understand it. Revel in the imagery and mystery of this great story—God's story.

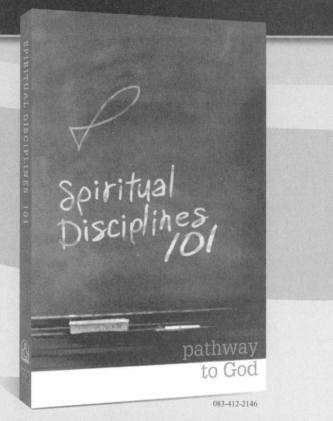

Experience Greater Intimacy With God!

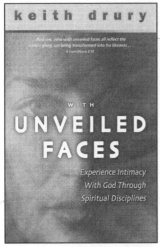

0-89827-298-X   **$12.99**
Paperback   160 pages

With Unveiled Faces

Experience Intimacy With God Through Spiritual Disciplines

By Keith Drury

Excellent for small group, Sunday school or personal study!

Nurture your relationship with God as you experience each of these personal spiritual disciplines:

- Prayer
- Silence
- Study
- Fasting
- Obedience
- Simplicity
- Giving
- Sacrifice
- Serving
- Meditation
- Journaling
- Self-denial
- Solitude

Each chapter of the book introduces the discipline, explains the biblical background, gives practical tips for practicing the discipline, and ends with questions for discussion and follow up.

Order today from your local Christian bookstore!

KEITH DRURY teaches practical ministry at Indiana Wesleyan University (Marion, Indiana). He has been a pastor, denominational leader, author, and conference speaker.